"Common Cents" vol. 2:

"Common Cents" vol. 2:

On the Growing Aristocracy,
a Synopsis/Compilation

Philip A. Bralich, PhD

BALBOA.
PRESS

A DIVISION OF HAY HOUSE

Balboa Press books may be ordered through booksellers or by contacting:

Balboa Press
A Division of Hay House
1663 Liberty Drive
Bloomington, IN 47403
www.balboapress.com
1-(877) 407-4847

Because of the dynamic nature of the Internet, any web addresses or links contained in this book may have changed since publication and may no longer be valid. The views expressed in this work solely those of the author and do not necessarily reflect the views of the publisher, and the publisher hereby disclaims any responsibility for them.

The author of this book does not dispense medical advice or prescribe the use of any technique as a form of treatment for physical, emotional, or medical problems without the advice of a physician, either directly or indirectly. The intent of the author is only to offer information of a general nature to help you in your quest for emotional and spiritual well-being. In the event you use any of the information in this book for yourself, which is your constitutional right, the author and the publisher assume no responsibility for your actions.

Any people depicted in stock imagery provided by Thinkstock are models, and such images are being used for illustrative purposes only.
Certain stock imagery © Thinkstock.

Printed in the United States of America

ISBN: 978-1-4525-7001-3 (sc)
ISBN: 978-1-4525-7002-0 (e)

Library of Congress Control Number: 2012907635

Balboa Press rev. date: 3/13/2013

TABLE OF CONTENTS

Is the King of Kings a Monarchist?

On Destroying the Creeping the Creeping Red Aristocracy, a Synopsis

Taxation w/out Representation is STILL Tyranny. Even if it is done by the "welcome benevolent conquerors" of the creeping red Aristocracy (the privileged, MBAs, and Lawyers).

CORE STATEMENT

On the Family of Four Income:

http://philipbralich.authorsxpress.com/2012/08/15/from-taxtherichdotname-on-the-family-of-four-income/

From TaxTheRichDotName: On the Family of Four Income

Posted on August 15, 2012

Taxation w/out representation is tryanny!

(even if it is from the priviledged, MBAs & lawyers)

On the Family of Four Income

Growing up in a lower, middle-class family in the mid-west, my parents and other adults were all aware of the family of four income and what jobs and college majors would likely provide such an income. There was little interest in jobs that paid millions, but great interest in jobs that allowed you to raise a family, own a house and a car in a safe neighborhood with good schools, a hospital, a church and convenient shopping. In fact, an interest in wealth beyond that was considered tawdry at best and dismissed with lines such as, "We don't want that kind of money."

This was an outgrowth of the efforts of the World War II generation who came home from war to create an economy that included jobs with family of four incomes, security, 40-hour work weeks, vacations, insurance, retirement, pension plans, and social security. They provided good schools, immunizations and doctor's checkups for their kids, and they saw pets and family vacations as important to raising children. They also supported unions to help guarantee the whole family of four system. My father would leave work decisively everyday at five to go home for dinner and take care of his family. We always expected him at six minutes after five. His insistence on leaving not earlier or later than five was part of the discipline that the World War II generation agreed was necessary to create the family of four economy. It was not "greed is good": it was good-hearted and family oriented. It was the true right wing. The right wing that people feel nostalgia for that was destroyed by Reagan and the broken right wing that has followed him. It was not the right wing that would bury the family of four income and attack job security, 40-hour work weeks, vacations, insurance, retirement, pension plans, and social security. It was a generation that kept a wary eye on the wealthy, recognizing the sneers, spin and frozen countenances of the greedy.

Since Reagan all of that has diminished significantly as the wealthy have continued to take more and more family of four incomes out of their companies, their communities, and U.S. economy and put it in the pockets of the upper 10%. There is no excuse for it. It is not based on family values; it is not based on the family of four income; it is based on personal greed. Trickle down is as much of a joke to them as is the claim that cutting the taxes for the rich will create jobs. Both are snide dismissals of a thinking public who recognize that trickle down and cutting the taxes on the rich are merely more hands in their pockets taking away the wealth that they have rightfully earned and which deserves to go to their families.

Let's assume for the sake of easy math that a family of four income is $50,000 per year. With that figure in mind, we can note that each $100,000 executive bonus takes 2 family of four incomes out of the company, the community, and U.S. economy. Every seven figure annual income takes 20 family of four incomes out of the company, the community, and the U.S. economy every year. Every nine figure annual income takes 200 family of four incomes out of the company, the community, and the U.S. economy every year. One $25,000,000 severance package for failed performance takes 500 family of four incomes out of the company, the community and the U.S. economy every time.

The presence of ATM's saved banks billions in salary packages and yet rather than paying us 50 cents each time we use it, they charge us instead and think that we are unaware of the guile behind this. There are countless examples of the shiftless, cunning, conning mentality of the broken right wing but little as yet that we can do about it. They turn to us and say we are going to have to take cuts in Medicare and the minimum wage and shamelessly turn around and give themselves millions in bonuses for having done so. They turn to us and say, like Herman Cain, "Don't complain. Go out and get a job and earn your wealth." This jaded, sadistic dig is just one of many that are eating at the hearts of the American public. The wealthy look, act, walk and talk like perps and pimps because they are. Their targets, the American family, look, act, walk and talk like vics because they are.

They aren't that good. We are. They did not provide the talent, creativity, hard work, inventiveness, and social skills necessary to run a business. We did. They merely developed a set of financial tools to wrench the profits from us and line their own pockets. They lower the wages, remove benefits, raise our fees and then when we have the audacity to say my child needs a doctor or my grandfather is bedridden, and I can no longer care for him, they say, "You should have thought of that earlier. You should have worked harder." And then for the brilliance of those rejoinders, they give themselves another million dollar bonus and create a 9 figure income for a crony.

They are not making this wealth, they are taking it, and it is time to take it back. They do not grow their companies, their communities, or the U.S. economy: in fact the problems in America today are precisely the result of this shift in the distribution of wealth and this destruction of the inventor, the talent and the creative, and it is attributable to one thing and one thing alone: the greed of today's wealthy and their inability to make judgments about anything other than the size of their wallets and their next bonus. They could see Social Security running at a profit if they did not see a huge sum of money that they could transfer into their own pockets. They could realize that government jobs are good jobs if they did not see the government payroll as a target. If they did not have their hands and minds on everybody else's wealth, they could see that local, state and federal governments would be far more interested in creating jobs with family of four incomes than the wealthy would ever be. There would be no mansions or yachts to pay for if the government were creating the jobs. The right wing has gone so far off track as to see themselves as the new fascists and liberals as the new non–Aryans. Jesus Christ was a liberal, and we are all sure that he still believes in giving to the poor, not creating them. The family of four income represents a distribution of wealth that would be expected of a Christian country. The current distribution of wealth looks like the Rome of Christ's time more than anything that developed out of Christianity.

The frustration of the American voting public is profound and justified and the occupy movements indicate the mere tip of an iceberg of a growing mass movement to get jobs, houses, and families back from the broken right wing that took it, the evil broken right wing that took it.

Fortunately, there is a solution at hand to return the distribution of wealth to the way it was in the 50's: we simply need to surtax the rich. President Obama currently has a 5.6% surtax the rich bill on the table, and we can look at this as a good start that hits exactly the right note. We can surtax them to pay the national debt; we can surtax them to fix social security; we can surtax them to put student grants and loans back on the table to the levels they were in the 70's. we can surtax them again and again and again until the wealthy sit-up straight, fold their hands nicely on the table, admit they were wrong, and put the money back. We can also be sure that a surtax the rich bill is as easily available and as easily implemented as a draft bill. The former to defend us from the rich who have demonstrated they can become internal enemies and the latter to defend us from external enemies.

There is no need for discussion or debate: this not about a fair tax. It is punitive. We can make or break the 2012 election around the surtax. President Obama has one ready to go. How about the family values right wing (not the broken right wing)?

When they say to us "Who's going to pay for this?" We're going to turn to them and say, " You are!" and then press the voting button for the surtax.

Sincerely,

Philip A. Bralich, Ph.D.

Give me liberty or give me debt: It is easier this go around.

GENERAL
POLITICAL
THEORY

http://philipbralich.authorsxpress.com/2012/08/11/how-to-
defeat-communism-and-fascism-worldwide-once-and-for-all/

How to Defeat Communism and Fascism Worldwide & Once and For All

Posted on August 11, 2012

Tax the rich thoroughly, profoundly, and punitively.

Make or Break the 2012!

How to Defeat Communism and Fascism World-Wide and Once and For All and Rediscover a True Free-Market Economy

The term "Capital" and the follow-on, "capitalism" and "communism" were coined by Marx to express his erroneous understanding of

Hegel. In particular, he took a particularly rigid scientific point of view of and accounted for the sense of alienation that comes from industrialization, modern science, and a growing society of workers (rather than farmers and serfs) with the view that in the modern view all of one's efforts can be seen as "labor." The soulless, spiritless, scientific automaton called man seeks to maintain and provide for himself via 5-senses efforts in the five-senses new-world of modern science. As oneself as laborer and one's goods and services as the output of labor become a commodity, the individual feels alienated from himself and his goods and services and is prey to those who would "take charge" of, own, and monopolize capital the externalized, alienated laborer and his goods and services. (One can often recognize this sense of alienation as a desperate need to cling at and manipulate a very unscientific psychological model of oneself and ones world at the chest of oneself and others and battle of trying to dig at and be in charge of one's own and others capital in that model.)

Political and philosophical writers of the time all recognized and discussed this sense of alienation but, unlike Marx, Hegel saw a philosophical solution to it. Marx, however, saw it as inevitable and requiring a political response rather than a philosophical one. His response was a collectivist one where the laborers as a group could wrest their capital back from the capitalists via an immediate and violent revolution and redistribute the wealth equally. "Capitalist" was meant to refer to all of monarchs, aristocrats, and industrialists and the terms capitalism and communism were meant to be taken as a novel insight into the problem and as the source of a solution, a collectivist one, that would revolutionize politics and economics.

Hegel, however, was able to offer a logical (philosophical or psychological) solution through a recognition of both the sense of alienation and its alternation with personal growth ("becoming"). As long as one is focused on self-development (for Hegel, through logic), the sense of alienation will alternate with a sense of a return to self. The closer one gets to an understanding of "absolute spirit," the closer that alternation comes to being an immediate mediation between alienation and becoming.) As a bi-product of this, those who are truly productive and improving their skills will not feel or fear the alienation, while those who are unproductive, lazy and regressive will turn all their efforts toward addressing the alienation in the politics and economy rather than in one's own psychology.

A Free Market economy has nothing to do with either Capitalism (the centralization of wealth in owners aristocrats or monarchs) or Communism (the equal distribution of wealth independent of considerations of individual contribution) because it is rooted in recognizing the individual's contribution in offering himself as laborer and his labor or goods to the market as well as its return from alienation in growth or "becoming" or financial compensation as his payment. A free market does not seek to manipulate or control just one side of the market, the sense of alienation but both sides the alienated laborer, goods, and services as well as the development of the individual and his skills, which fosters the return from alienation, fair compensation, the development of the worker, and economy based on individual self development and production rather than one based on collectivism. The individual is like a numerator which defines and determines the fraction, while collectivism is the denominator, the term under discussion. A collectivist society always regresses to primitivity as it requires and ever-growing lowest common denominator to maintain itself. As seen with every communist country in the world this constant lowering of the bar is a slow, painful, and inevitable regression into primitivity. Two of the clearest examples of this are North Korea and Cuba, who simply cannot lift themselves out poverty as they cannot respect individual effort or contribution. Worse, they also have a tendency to take credit for individual and novel effort, claiming that the collectivists, who by definition cannot innovate are the true innovators and the individual some kind of a thief. This is why the gulags are filled with poets and inventors, the true creatives.

Marx also did not understand democracy or the vote. Even in the impossible event that Marx were correct, ensuring, supporting, and developing the vote could achieve all his economic goals. However, this would be impossible in his eyes because the vote guarantees individual effort at the expense of the collective, the lowest common denominator.

Capitalism in America is a failed free market because like all Marxism it is based on the alienation of oneself as a worker and of ones products and services and the everyman for himself money grubbing grab for that alienated wealth is all the results. The collectivist cultures seek to redress the problem from the side of "the people" while the individualist side of the problem seeks to redress the problem through the money grab for capital. Respect for a genuine evalution of the contribution of the individual is lost in the demeaning of ones work into every lowering minimum wage and a lauding of the most successful and most unaccountable money grubbers.

Maoism wallows in the same error as Marx but uses a different kind of revolution to rectify the problem. The Maoist revolution, rather than being overt, direct, and immediate is a prolonged, covert, "guerilla" revolution where the peasants, with or without guns, wherever they may be or whatever they may doing are constantly taking "one more step" into the wealth and the confidence of the nobles, the holders of the capital. This has morphed into a system where anyone who is not of the collective, "the Borg" if you will, is a threat, a noble, and selfish miscreant and all of the peasants will see them as targets to be "stepped into" and absorbed with a cocked back head, a stupid toothy grin, and a shilling lie for the infidel.

Let's hope Marx's misunderstanding was not an expeditious one meant to leave the card holding leaders of the movement with "the goods" from either side of Marxism, capitalism or communism via their recognition of the alternation of personal growth and alienation.

Both sides of Marxist, the capitalists and the communists, must continually foster that sense of alienation through heightening on the dependence on the collective and the inevitable, "sad-but-true" truth of the alienation, man as spiritless, soulless automaton.

There may be a tongue in cheek "secret" recognition of what Hegel actually meant that is shared among the leaders i.e. the alternation of alienation and personal growth. In getting the masses to focus on the alienation and to toss out there interest in personal growth, substituting it for dependence on their revolutionary leaders, they are totally lost in that alienation, the wealth goes to the communist leaders and the masses are left with toothy grins, bobbing heads, and a shiney new bell for his bicycle no matter what his efforts may be. He will also think, like a redneck buying scrathers, that confidence in his alienation will any day now turn into massive wealth. The masses further throw up their arms, surrender to their leaders even surrender their souls to their leaders the more the masses also give up on the sense that personal, individual growth is anything but selfishness.

A true democracy and a vote destroys the collective, builds the free market and the individual, and fosters the return from alienation that neither capitalists nor communists can tolerate.

A true solution to both sides of the Marxist dynamic is a bill to tax the rich. The voter can and has a responsibility to redress the distribution of wealth via an assertion of individual growth as a vote to tax the rich. Because the Marxists in America (those on the capitalist side) have gotten in so deeply, it is crucial to tax them hard, fast, repeatedly, and punitively until the capitalists understand the individual and the free market, not the manipulation of the alienation of the automaton is the authority in the county.

The voter must tax them thoroughly, profoundly, and repeatedly until they sit up straight, fold their hands on the table, admit they were wrong, apologize, and PUT THE MONEY BACK! And they need to be taxed again and again and again until the history books read that the Marxists, the capitalists, succumbed and made restitution. And further tax then again and again and again until the voter always has a tax the rich bill at the ready should the Marxists once again raise their heads and their gooky, digging hands to attack, gouge and violate the individual.

This effort would also be a true peace movement as it would take war out of the hands of the wealthy and place it in the control of military strategy, politicians, and the voter.

Sincerely,

Philip A. Bralich, Ph.D.

Give me liberty or give me debt: It is easier this go around.

ON THE FREE MARKET VERSUS CAPITALISM:

http://philipbralich.authorsxpress.com/2012/09/07/
on-the-free-market-vs-capitalism/

← Previous Next →

From TaxTheRichDotName: On the Free Market VS Capitalism

Posted on September 7, 2012

How to Defeat Communism and Fascism World-Wide and Once and For All and Rediscover a True Free-Market Economy via a Proper Understanding of Hegel

The term "Capital" and the follow-on, "capitalism" and "communism" are terms coined by Marx to express his erroneous understanding of Hegel and his description of a philosophical solution that can solve the problem of the loss of faith in religion brought on by modern science. Hegel and many other writers of the time pointed out a widespread sense of alienation due to that loss of faith and confusion concerning the "death of God" and the obvious advances of science.

In particular, Marx took a singularly rigid scientific point of view of and accounted for that sense of alienation that comes from industrialization, modern science, and a growing society of workers (rather than believers, farmers and serfs) with the view that in the modern scientific view all of man's efforts can be seen as "labor": the soulless, spiritless, scientific automaton called man seeks to maintain and provide for himself via 5-senses efforts in the five-senses new-world of modern science. As oneself as laborer and one's goods and services as the output of labor become a commodity, the individual feels alienated from himself and his goods and services and is prey to those who would "take charge" of, own, and monopolize "capital," the externalized, alienated laborer and his goods and services. (One can often recognize this sense of alienation as a desperate need to cling at and manipulate a very unscientific, psychological model of oneself and ones world at the chest of oneself and others and a desperate battle of trying to dig at and be in charge of one's own and others capital in that model.)

Political and philosophical writers of Marx's time all recognized and discussed this sense of alienation but, unlike Marx, Hegel saw a philosophical solution to it. Marx saw it as inevitable and requiring a political response rather than a philosophical one. His response was a collectivist one where the laborers as a group could wrest their capital, their alienation, back from the capitalists via an immediate and violent revolution and redistribute the wealth equally through a collective, "communist," unified effort. "Capitalist" was meant to refer to all of monarchs, aristocrats, and industrialists, and the terms capitalism and communism were meant to be taken as a novel insight into the reality of man's new scientific condition recognized as a soulless, spiritless, automaton seeking to find his way in the world of the five senses via the five senses. The solution he offered, a political one, was one that did not require a philosophical (psychological) effort but a collectivist one, a solution that would revolutionize politics and economics through the efforts of the alienated masses.

Hegel, however, was able to offer a logical (philosophical or psychological) solution through a recognition of both the sense of alienation and its alternation with personal growth ("becoming"). As long as one is focused on self-development (for Hegel, through logic), the sense of alienation will alternate with a sense of a return to self. The closer one gets to an understanding of "absolute spirit" (Godhead, enlightenment, salvation, sainthood, Unus Mundus, etc.) the closer that alternation comes to being an immediate mediation between alienation and becoming. As a bi-product of this, those who are truly productive and improving their skills will not feel or fear the alienation, while those who are unproductive, lazy and regressive will turn all their efforts toward addressing the alienation in the politics and economy rather than in one's own psychology.

The whole problem which motivated Marx to see the world as one of capitalists versus communists was the alienation of oneself, one's efforts, and one's goods and services and the desperate need to get back the alienated self, goods, and services. Marx had no sense of the alternation of alienation and personal growth and saw the alienation as a problem of the masses versus the industrialists who were manipulating, dominating, and taking the alienated workers and goods and services.

What Marx did not understand was a free a market. A Free Market economy has nothing to do with either Capitalism (the centralization of wealth in owners, industrialists, aristocrats or monarchs) or Communism (the equal distribution of wealth independent of considerations of individual contribution) because it is rooted in recognizing the alternation of alienation and becoming (personal growth). The individual's contribution in offering himself as laborer and his labor or goods to the market as well as receiving its return from alienation in growth or "becoming" or financial compensation as his payment is the basis of a free market. Both capitalism and communism are Marxist and collectivist and refuse to recognize individual effort and growth. A free market does not seek to manipulate or control just one side of the market, the sense of alienation and its result, but both sides: the alienated laborer, goods, and services as well as the development of the individual and his skills, which fosters the return from alienation, fair compensation, the development of the worker, and economy based on individual self development and production rather than one based on collectivism.

The individual is like a numerator which defines and determines a fraction, while collectivism is the denominator, the term under discussion. A collectivist society is a denominator which always regresses to primitivity as it requires an ever-growing **lowest common** denominator to maintain itself. As seen with every communist country in the world, this constant lowering of the bar is a slow, painful, and inevitable regression into primitivity. Two of the clearest examples of this are North Korea and Cuba, who simply cannot lift themselves out poverty as they cannot respect individual effort or contribution. Worse, they also have a tendency to take credit for individual and novel effort, claiming that the collectivists, who by definition cannot innovate are the true innovators and the individual some kind of a thief. This is why the gulags are filled with poets and inventors, the true creatives.

Russia finally conceded its years of failures and acquiesced to the superiority of individualism present in the success of the U.S. and Western Europe. China has begun to change in spite of its nod toward communism through its further and further acceptance of a true free market, one which respects the individual. South America and pretty much any culture which has accepted the Marxist principal of a collectivist solution continues that slow painful regression into primitivity.

A good way to see the difference between a free market economy and a Marxist one is to look at the entertainment industry versus American Marxism, those who want to be on the receiving side, the capitalist side, the Marxist dynamic. In the entertainment industry (for the most part anyway), the talent, skills, and experience of the individual drives the profits, not the manipulation of laborers as a group and their output. The more the capitalists drive the industry the greater the failure. Marxism, for both capitalists and communists, is contrary to individualism and contrary to talent, skills, and experience. This is how we know that those at the top of a Marxist food chain are master manipulators of others output not contributors of any sort; they are like Lucifers who take credit for and the profits from the Creators.

n.b. There are no great Marxist or Maoist or collectivist films – talent is individual and not collective. Marxism on both sides (capitalism and communism) pretends consensus will out but there never has been nor where there ever be a true consensus. Consensus is always a bitter pretense and nodding smile toward the loss of one/s personal efforts and an acquiescence to a plurality one cannot overcome. Without the talent there are no profits. Marxism mitigates against individualism, fosters consensus and the lowest common denominator and thereby mitigates against success. Collectivism and consensus always lead to cunning, passive aggressive undermining, and huffy pretense.

Marx also did not understand democracy or the vote. Even in the impossible event that Marx were correct, ensuring, supporting, and developing the vote could achieve all his economic goals through merely voting the money out of the hands of the capitalists and into those of the workers. However, this would be impossible in his eyes because the vote guarantees individual effort at the expense of the collective, the lowest common denominator.

Capitalism in America is a failed free market because like all Marxism it is based on the alienation of oneself as a worker and of ones products and services and the everyman for himself money grubbing grab for that alienated wealth is all the results. The capitalist is NOT the most innovative or the most productive: the capitalist is the one most likely to foster, control, and take advantage of the sense of alienation and to encourage it as inevitable result of the modern scientific mind. The individual, the creative, is marginalized and the alienated are forced into dependence on the capitalist and his willingness to degrade individualism and personal growth and encourage the collectivism and consensus he can take advantage of. The collectivist cultures seek to redress the problem from the side of "taking care of" the masses, "the people," via their money grab, while the individualist, free market, side of the problem seeks to redress the problem through the encouragement of and development of individual skills, experience, and talent and a proper recompense for that rather than for manipulation. Respect for a genuine evalution of the contribution of the individual is lost in the demeaning of one's work into the ever lowering minimum wage and a lauding of the most wealthy and most unaccountable money grubbers. The "he who dies with the most money wins" mentality.

Maoism wallows in the same error as Marx but uses a different kind of revolution to rectify the problem. The Maoist revolution, rather than being overt, direct, and immediate is a prolonged, covert, "guerilla" revolution where the peasants, with or without guns, wherever they may be or whatever they may doing are constantly taking "one more step" into the wealth and the confidence of the nobles, the holders of the capital. This has morphed into a system where anyone who is not of the collective, "the Borg" if you will, is a threat, a noble, and a selfish miscreant, and all of the peasants will see them as targets to be "stepped into" and absorbed with a cocked back head, a stupid toothy grin, and a shilling lie for the infidel (the individual). Metaphorically, Marxist revolutionariess can be seen as locusts devouring the fields of the "capital" of centuries of civilization (e.g. *Independence Day*, the movie), while Maoist revolutionaries can be seen as cockroaches moving in to the homes of the nobles (the individuals) to devour the goods of those who have understood and can participate in centuries of civilization, the alternation of personal growth and alienation. The movie *Zombieland* is a good example of the Maosit mentality, where the individuals are constantly beleaguered by the undead cannibals.

Thus, both capitalism and communism are both Marxist concepts and both mitigate against individualism and growth. Let's hope Marx's misunderstanding was not an expeditious one meant to leave the card holding leaders of the movement with "the goods" of the immediate mediation of becoming and alienation, while leaving the masses AND the capitalists with the sense of alienation and the never ending battle of consensus and the threat of the individual and the free market.

Both sides of Marxism, the capitalists and the communists, must continually foster that sense of alienation through heightening the dependence on the collective and the "inevitable, sad-but-true" truth of the alienation, man as spiritless, soulless automaton.

That is, let's hope there is not a tongue in cheek "secret" recognition of what Hegel actually meant that is shared among the leaders (the recognition of the alternation of alienation and personal growth). In getting the masses to focus on the alienation and to toss out their interest in personal growth in the name of consensus and substituting it for dependence on their revolutionary leaders, they are totally lost in that alienation. The wealth then goes to the Marxist leaders and the masses are left with toothy grins, bobbing heads, and a shiney new bell for their bicycles no matter what their efforts may be. They will also think, like a redneck buying scrathers, that confidence in this alienation and the good will of the Marxist leaders will any day now turn into massive wealth as the "thieving individuals" are placed in the gulags. The more the masses further throw up their arms in the face of alienation and the dependency it fosters and the more they surrender to their leaders and even surrender their souls to their leaders, the more the masses also give up on the sense that personal, individual growth is anything but selfishness.

A true democracy and a vote destroys the collective, builds the free market and the individual, and fosters the return from alienation that Marxists (both capitalists and communists) can tolerate.

A true solution to both sides of the Marxist dynamic is merely to tax the rich via the vote. There is no reason to kill the rich, oppress the poor, or imprison the individual. The voter can and has a responsibility to redress the distribution of wealth via an assertion of individual growth as a vote to tax the rich. Because the Marxists in America (those on the capitalist side, those who love Marxism but want to be on the receiving side) have gotten in so deeply, it is crucial to tax them hard, fast, repeatedly, and punitively until the Marxist capitalists understand that the individual and the free market, not the manipulation of the alienation of the automaton is the true authority in the county.

In order to return to the free market envisioned by our forefathers, the voter must tax the capitalists thoroughly, profoundly, and repeatedly until they sit up straight, fold their hands on the table, admit they were wrong, apologize, and put the money back. And they need to be taxed again and again and again until the history books read that the Marxists, the capitalists, succumbed and made restitution. And further, the voter must tax them again and again and again until the voter always has a tax the rich bill at the ready should the Marxists once again raise their heads and their gooky, digging hands to attack, gouge and violate the individual via their capitalism.

This effort would also be a true peace movement as it would take war out of the hands of the wealthy and place it in the control of military strategy, politicians, and the voter.

Sincerely,

Philip A. Bralich, Ph.D.

Give me liberty or give me debt: It is easier this go around.

Is the King of Kings a Monarchist:

http://philipbralich.authorsxpress.com/2012/08/12/
is-the-king-of-kings-a-monarchist/

Is the King of Kings a Monarchist?

Posted on August 12, 2012

Was Jesus Christ, the King of Kings, a Monarchist?

"In a time of ignorance, one has no doubts even while doing the greatest evils [power politics, political expeditiousness, spin]; in an enlightened age, one trembles even while doing the greatest goods [the Declaration, the Constitution, the Bill of Rights]. One feels the old abuses and sees their correction, but one also sees the abuses of the correction itself."

– *L'Esprit des Lois* ("The Spirit of the Laws"), Montesquieu, Charles de Secondat, baron de 1748.

(This book was banned by the Catholic Church at the time of its first appearance. Perhaps it is still today. Whatever the reason, this is an important thing to consider as a glib dismissal of nihil obstat and imprimatur by those who cannot earn them undercuts the wisdom and warning that may underlie their refusal as well as those who would take them seriously. I am not sure but suspect the reason is that Montesquieu was not sufficiently aware of and inclusive of divine law and nature's law. He seems primarily to deal with man's law and ignores both nature's law and God's law or at least does not go into them in any detail beyond the above quote. Specifically, he only deals with monarchy and does not delve much into the issue of divine-right monarchy or enlightened monarchy. So bearing that in mind and wanting to keep the Catholics on board, his book needs to be viewed from the perspective of a possible gap here and the need at some point to include a discussion of divine right monarchy or "enlightened monarchy" both of which would keep "the higher intelligence of the primordial soup from which all life and later government arises," God, in the discussion.)

That being said, Was Jesus Christ, the King of Kings, a Monarchist?

In a democracy erected by Christians in a time of religious oppression, largely from the monarchies but also from and between different denominations since the beginning of the Protestant Reformation and from other religions, we must wonder if either the Divine Right Governmental Monarchies and the Ecclesiastical monarchy of the Pope were correct in their oppression or whether the Protestant Revolution (any one of which had the potential to be as oppressive as the monarchies or the Papacy) or the founding fathers were. This is hardly a question that has been resolved in a general and widely accepted way, though particular Christian denominations and political movements may assert that it has been resolved, and they assert that it has been resolved via their particular solution.

There is a current frustration with the today's government, there is nostalgia among many Catholics for the Papacy and perhaps also for Divine Right Monarchy, and there are still urresolved issues of the ideal government for the U.S. for the West, and perhaps anywhere in the world. There are those who long for communism or socialism, others for a completely unbridled and unaccountable capitalist aristocracy, and yet others for a return to Divine Right Christian monarchy. Underlying all this is a centuries old commitment to Christianity as well as a nearly century old commitment to no religion at all and the conflict that entails.

But as the centuries old commitment to Christ and Christianity drives much of the conversation, we must ask, "Was Jesus Christ, the King of Kings, a Monarchist?" We might further ask if in our interest in freedom, the removal of oppression, and the belief in the excesses of the Papacy, led us to throw out the baby (the Renaissance, the Vatican, the Baroque, centuries of traditions, Opera, and so forth) with the bathwater of an oppression that could not keep up with the development of the mind of man and the desire for freedom? Certainly, these movements were large and in many ways effective but few (except perhaps for some of the most rabid Modernist artists and some communists longing for the world of the serfs of the peasant revolution) would advocate the dismantling or the removal of our greatest traditions and monuments nor would they advocate the outlawing of symphonies, artists that can actually draw a nose or sculpt the human form or piano teachers.

So it seems, that a central and crucial question to ask is, "Was the King of Kings a monarchist?" And if he was, where does today's democracy and Christianity fit in? Peripheral questions include did we somehow supplant, surpass, or outgrow the King of Kings himself, the Son of the higher intelligence of the primordial soup from which all life and government arises (God). Are we questioning His divinity, have we given up on His return, or has He taken too long to return and now we must start over? Has our frustration in waiting for the glorious return left us bitter, disheartened and wondering what precisely was the end of the era he was talking about? The rain of Herod, 100 years, 500 years, 1000 years, Pisces? Did science truly convince us that Jesus Christ and His story simply could not have happened even while we scientifically test and explore the miracles of the Tibetans and Hindus? Has science convinced us that an exploration of the primordial suit demonstrated that there is no intelligence there to be investigated and has the commonality of the story found in this myths of other religions demonstrated the untruth of them all rather than the need to explain the commonality of the belief and the mythological vision or lack thereof that convinces so many they are true?

We can note the existence of those peripheral questions and leave their resolution to later discussions, but threats to our current democracy, the one founded by those Christians seeking to prevent religious oppression for all, force us to consider whether or not the current form of can or should be questioned from a Christian point of view. Montesquieu can help us expand the discussion a bit.

Montesquieu argues that there are just three forms of government: monarchy, republic (aristocracy or democracy depending on who constitutes the voters), and despotism. He further argues that the driving force ("the spring") behind each is different: monarchy runs on honor, republic on love of country and equality, and despotism on fear. Given that the government of the time of Christ was driven by fear (torture, crucifixion, etc.) , we can conclude it was a time of despotism. His act of courage in walking into the arrest and trial in spite of his suffering brought down the despotism and with it torture and fear driven government. However, the governments that arose from His efforts for 1500+ years were monarchistic, driven by honor, the "Honor Thy Father and Mother" type of Honor.

Acts of courage destroy a despotism and we can be sure he was not a supporter of despotism, fear driven government or torture. Either a monarchy or a republic can arise from those acts of courage that destroy a despotism or a new despotism can try and reassert itself, but He was not around for further quotable comment except via mystical experience and the only clear dicta he gives for governing oneself and presumably others is "Love they neighbor as yourself," and "Do not unto others as you would have them do unto you," (this latter often being misunderstood as "Do unto others before they do unto you,") and "Give to the poor." Do these justify either or both of a monarchy or a democracy? At the risk of offending the Catholic church and the many monarchists that have followed, it is humbly offered that the spring of monarchy, "honor" seems much more suited to an Old Testament government while, Christ's dicta seem more suited to a republic but not to any republic but specifically to a democratic one, where one does unto others equally rather than unto the poor. The spring of monarchy, honor, is not disrupted by acts of courage but by the one thing it cannot handle, the honest man, the honest man who cannot be cheated or 'l'honnete homme" of Montesquieu's time (1750s). Christ's uncompromising honesty in the face of whatever he encountered is sufficient to demonstrate that he is not interested in the expeditious truth that is required of a monarchy that the monarch may make all the decisions and take all wealth and power from the people and distribute it as he sees fit in his role as caretaker or "Father" of the people who are controlled and commanded as he sees fit for the greater good of all.

Thus, it seems, at least given Montesquieu's arguments and Christ's dicta, conclude that Christ was not a monarchist, a despot, or an aristocrat but a democratist. We might also conclude that the word in the first century was not ready for a democracy nor the people sufficiently educated and well-fed to allow one, but we still must conclude that he was a democratist.

But does this force us to drop the title, "King of Kings"? Perhaps not, a democracy in some sense can be viewed as conglomeration of many monarchies where every man is the king of his castle and every woman a queen, and in their willingness to do unto others, to love one another, to give to the poor and to love one's neighbor, we honor Christ as the leader of this conglomeration of monarchs and the monarchs themselves respect each other via the love of country, freedom, and equality. And we remind one another that "equality" refers to equality under the law not an enforced and mindless equality that mitigates against, talent, hard work, genius or fortunate birth, good looks, or prowess, and we create laws that perfect and engender this equality.

Thus, while in principle we might say that the King of King's is a democratist not a monarchist but in our activity we preserve both the Honor of the old testament governments and the love of country and equality of the U.S. and other Western countries. This maintaining of both honor and equality means there is no need to fear the honest man (not even within our own families, our personal monarchies) nor as a threat to the country; we also need not fear the threat to equality, the coming of a sole monarchy or a despotism. We do yet need to worry about the arisal of an aristocracy as we see in the current abuses of capitalism, but this too can be mitigated by the King of King's via the dictum to give to the poor.

Our love of neighbor allows us to offer freedom or religion and speech to others and our devotion to Christ via the masons, the Protestants and the Catholics allows us to govern and maintain this complex state while adhering to the dicta of Christ.

Thus, we can conclude that Christ is a democratist economically and a monarchist from "above" from outside the system in one's faith and through that our ability maintain Old Testament Honor and New Testament divisions of wealth. We need only remove the tendency to aristocracy that a capitalism without consequences or accountability can bring, and all we need for that is further laws that guarantee the unalienable God given rights of all .

This last may yet need some work, but we may perhaps be able to find a solution in the criticisms of Marcuse who notes that neither capitalism nor communism have ever left a culture without too many poor.

Sincerely,

Philip A. Bralich, Ph.D.

Give me liberty or give me debt: It is easier this go around.

On a side note, in our good-hearted rush to live the words of the Christian faith we confuse the dictum to avoid pride, vanity, and sensuousness with a dictum to dumb down, ugly up, and gross out when in reality, we should stay with good self-esteem (neither over-bearing and "in-your-face" nor excessively self-deprecatory), healthy good lucks that encourage healthy dating behaviors, and a knees together, back straight, wholesomeness. Healthy is not nasty. Gross is not healthy. Those of marriageable age are fertile not sensual.

PROBLEMS ON THE LEFT

Il Fianco:

http://philipbralich.authorsxpress.com/2012/06/14/il-fianco-2/

← Previous Next →

Il Fianco

Posted on June 14, 2012

"Il fianco … ."

At first it was just like a murmuring breeze in the trees or the hopeful mouthing of words by children, but still you seemed to hear it… "Il fianco." It also seemed that others seemed to hear it, take note, and cautiously wonder if others had heard the same thing. Everyone wanted to think about it or ask about but it was not articulated quite loud enough and it was unclear from where or from whom it was coming … the devil, the avant garde, the Christian right…? God himself? A harbinger of the promise of the rising sun and the second coming? The age of Aquarius the long awaited age after the dawning of Pisces?

"Il fianco … ."

Yet the looks and the murmurs seemed to be hopeful and promising, you wanted to hear it again, you wanted to comment but could not, you wanted to try it yourself, "Il fianco … ." Just in a whisper, just in case, but you wanted to try it … "Il fianco."

Children took delight, warriors took heart, mothers breathed a long sigh of relief as though years of oppression would suddenly be lifted and children could once again play together safely and boys could go the neighboring field and form baseball teams.

The tension though was palpable again soon after, a promising spring wind after a long cold winter … just a momentary breeze or was the sun about to break through for the season?

Some could remember the breaking of spring which resulted in be-ins and flower children. The whole world and everyone seemed to be infected with the hope and promise of something warm to do, something creative and positive …

"il fianco … ."

But then an icy wind blew across the nation as the reality of a great noble experiment gone horribly wrong resulted in thousands of wondering homeless, schizophrenia taken as wisdom, and perversion and degradation everywhere.

"Il fianco … ."

It was still promising, but perhaps too soon. Perhaps it should be quieted, or perhaps we should wait and let it grow on its own. It was not possible to look to the breeze with mere hope and smiles and pleasant nods to neighbors you thought were forever lost. Might someone actually have a conversation rather than a competition? It was beautiful yet seductive and necessary to view it with trepidation. Was another icy wind about to blow on top of another noble experiment?

"Il fianco … ."

http://philipbralich.authorsxpress.com/2012/06/14/northbeach/

← Previous Next →

Report from North Beach

Posted on June 14, 2012

Report from North Beach SF on the Occassion of the Celebration of Jack Kerouac's Birthday

Looking to explore the atmosphere for books and art and wanting to attend the two-day, Jack Kerouac birthday celebration sponsored by the Beat Museum, I spent three days in North Beach. The atmosphere requires a bit more of a discussion, so I will describe the birthday celebration first.

On Sunday the 11th and Monday the 12th, the Beat Museum sponsored a celebration of Kerouac's 90th. The first night had a small reading a band called the "Dharma Bums" and an meeting with interview with Al Hinkle one of the original travelers with Jack in his *On the Road*. The meeting with Al Hinkle was the highlight, and we were able to purchase signed books as well as a photo with Al and Jack. There was wine and cake and we sat around in a combination of comfy chairs and folding chairs in the midst of all the beat memorabilia of the museum.

The next day was mostly readings and the passing of a scroll on which people made notes, attempted spontaneous poetry, or wrote congratulations. I was able to say something like, "To Jack on his 90th, something something, ... and I am glad Camus killed the existentialists in L'Etranger and made room for the Beats." In general, though they hardly know me, I suspect they find me a bit aggressive. Well, ... Tant pis as they say ... I have always been the guy who never really has anything good to say about anyone, so why stop at a Beat scroll. The highlight of the evening was a call from either New York or Paris from the actor in the upcoming movie version of *On the Road* by the guy who plays Neil Cassady. I understand that Jack's son was there and wondered if it wasn't the tall, good-looking, blond guy with the 50's haircut, pouring wine who you want to invite to parties because you know the good-looking girls will turn up if he is there, but I wasn't really sure and wouldn't ask of course. The poetry was pretty good and on-genre but the one that was most impressive was a guy in his late twenties or early thirties poeming out his time in prison with particularly insightful and revealing word-portraits of the harshness and bizarness of that life and his mind in there and now. He was new to reading in public, so he had difficulty finding the rhythm of the audience but he engaged, explained, and entertained none-the-less.

The North Beach Scene itself however is a study in contrasts. At one moment you think that Modernism, the Avant Garde and the Beat are dead and all that is left is this neighborhood monument to a time of hope, but then an old guy in a pork pie hat, a four-day growth of beard and a long black coat who you didn't really notice you looks at you with a mild impatience and goes back about his way. City Lights seems to be thriving but as tight as a republican saying grace though the comfy chairs and the invite to sit down and read are still there. Jack Kerouac Alley and Vesuvio's maintain their charm and promise but there is an extra layer of dust, more than you would think that comes from merely ignoring the housework because the conversation is too good, that makes you think something is wrong.

Overall, there is hope for the future of art, even modern art and modernism, and more than the hope that "art will out" no matter what obstacles are placed in its way a hope that seems the last flickers could still generate a fire. But you can't look around without feeling that the avant-garde has been devoured by its own devotion and committment. A desire to shock the complaceny of the bourgeoisie in art and politics through asserting the now as a more creative and unbeatable response to the traditional that left the artist surrounded by the high fashioned sycophants praising his art and blaming and disdaining the artist, the central figure of the world of art, for at one minute being an attention seeking vampire who got all his ideas from their creativity and harassment and in the next saying they are stealing his art because he just won't share, has merely resulted in a soi-disant, nouvell bougeoise, a derriere ouvert, that do the same with bad clothes and no manners. Wherever you go, whether it be bars, coffee shops, restaurants and shops, the artist is immediately recognized by his being surrounded and harassed by both the vielle bourgeoisie and the derriere ouvert. The derrier ouvert all think they are the artists and like the vielle bourgeoisie, the see the artist alternately as an attention seeking vampire who doesn't deserve all the good ideas fed to him by them and as a creative genius who just won't share and therefore must be vampirized for his ideas and for his unwillingness to participate in the derriere ouvert. When they succeed in doing something themselves, which is rare because they have no talent, no drive and no insight and must desperately occupy themselves with true artists to feel any sense of life at all. When they create, we find the twisted, gnarled and rusted statue in a boutique window with the label "Nude on a beach," which with a closer viewing will shout, "My God what have we done. Why can't we stop ourselves? Why can't we stop ourselves?" And before that realization reaches the mind of the perpetrator of that disaster, he turns quickly away puts on the shit-eating grin of false pride and retreats to his mutual admiration society, a society of friends with no other criteria for association but disdain for the true artist and true art and they seek out in groups to find one for they do not like each other and they do not like anyone else very much but they can manage to get along by uniting in surrounding a common target, the artist, and harassing him/her either to suicide or homelessness. This is the way of both the vielle bourgeoisie and the derriere ouvert, two versions of the same thing, no talent sycophants, one in the latest fashion and mannerly (to a point), the other ill-mannered and poorly dressed.

Modernism and the avant garde have spawned this derriere ouvert of sycophantic pretenders and has no idea what to do with them and this inability to recognize that there efforts merely transformed the vielle ouvert into the derriere ouvert have frozen the entire situation. This frozenness if further exacerbated by the staleness, the rigidity and the lack of imagination contained within the idea that newness and shock were the only way to do true art. Nowness and shock can only lead to a pointless downward spiral into the spinning whirlpool of a latrine because it refuses to recognize the only possible result is a nihilistic emptiness where everything and everyone becomes the traditional and are themselves open for the criticisms of the yet newer newness and the shock that they have coming for having become the traditional. This fundamental weakness was asserted as a strength very early on by "Theophile Gaurier (1811-1872), poet, novelist, reviewer, the most quotable advocate of art for art's sake, who said, 'Nothing is truly beautiful but what can never be of no use to anything. Everything that is useful is ugly, for it is the expression of some need, and human needs are ignoble and disgusting, like men's own poor and feeble nature. The most useful place in a home is a latrine," (Quoted in Peter Gay's *Modernism*). So in his disdain for traditional art and its focus on beauty, he helped demonstrate the central failure in the avant garde, the unstoppable advance into the eddy of the latrine and the arrival of the derreire ouvert.

There is hope, the flickers are still there, but nothing but a working class traditionalism could possible move the 5500+ history of art forward before it goes down the latrine of modernism.

Philip A. Bralich, Ph.D.

P.S. For the record, there are modernists which escaped this problem, to name a few: Freud, his inner circle, his daughter Anna Freud, Melanie Klein, many object relations theorists, Jung, Adler and many of their followers, Rodin, Mucha, Nouveau, the Surrealists, the Impressionists perhaps but my appreciation of them often feels like a growing false enthusiasm that indicates that one is being drawn into a con game.

Problems on the Right

PORTRAIT OF A SATANIST:

http://www.mmdnewswire.com/taxtherichdotname-portrait-of-a-satanist-85186.html

- <u>Skip to content</u>
- <u>Skip to main navigation</u>
- <u>Skip to 1st column</u>
- <u>Skip to 2nd column</u>

MMD Newswire: Press Release News Wire

- Latest Press Releases
- Search
- Writing Help
- Press Release Distribution
- Most Popular Headlines
- ◌˄
- ◌˭
- ◌˅

From TaxTheRichDotName: Portrait of a Satanist

E-mail | Print | PDF

January 27, 2012 (MMD Newswire) -- Available for reprint as Op Ed:

Tax the rich thoroughly, profoundly, and punitively. http://www.taxtherich.name

Portrait of a Satanist

"The only one-word synonym for 'evil' is 'control'." Quoted by C.G. Jung.

Control is the dynamic that drives oppression and dominance and stifles freedom and is the first tool of choice of a Satanist, the first and foremost master of oppression. To recognize a Satanist, the first and primary symptom to look for is control, a need for control of others, not oneself. In addition, is the concomitant use of hypocrisy, denial, blame, and betrayal as well as "great deception" (spin), the main tools of the Great Deceiver himself. These are used as a spiritual "power." Used together, they are a truly, formidable, spiritual power, but one that comes with a red tail, bat wings and bat hands rather than Angel wings.

Many of today's pundits and policitians are particularly good examples of those who are skilled at Satanism, though the perversion of the right wing over the last 40 years and the lifestyle and strategy of the ultra rich is characterized by this dynamic as well. Kim Jong Il, his father, Mao, Pol Pot, Hitler, Stalin, Che etc., the entirety of the "stars" of the age of dictators as well as the despot kings of times past are other good examples. For the west, Hitler and his minister of propaganda, Goebbels, are perhaps the best examples and many of today's pundits and politicians are the best exemplars of this today, where the politician plays the role of Hitler and the pundit his spinning apologist. In this dynamic today, the right plays fascist to the liberal's non-Aryan outsider. Hegel agrees that history repeats, but for him, when it repeats, it repeats as a farce, we might add as a tragic farce. The current disparity in the distribution of wealth in the U.S. and elsewhere is the tragic farce repetition of the age of dictators.

To see this dynamic in operation, you need to think of it as the "Great Switcheroo" where the perp, the controlling politician and pundit, etc. asserts his/her faults through a reversal by blaming his vic (the liberals, the poor, foolish, dependent voters or anyone who challenges the perps) with precisely the faults of themselves and their cohort by visiting the sins of the evil father on the sons. Anytime they note a weakness in themselves, they assert these as those of their targets with bluster, insult, and cheap rhetoric. They then deny these faults in themselves and betray anyone who calls them on it with isolation, degradation, slander, firing and insult. Note particularly, the pundit who asserts his fairness and lack of bias and his decrial of spin and then demonizes the liberals with spin and rhetoric while accusing them of the same. Note also how these politicians and pundits use their bat hands to derail any logic that might challenge them, poking and gouging their hands and their pens at the left eye of their guest or the entire news audience and then pretend that of course they wouldn't do that on their own themselves, they are doing it for their adversaries as a favor because THE ADVERSARY is evil and too foolish to recognize it.

Other indicators of the presence of the Satanist is the tendency to use one's hands like the appendages of bat wings, to jut at adversaries with the hip in a manner that can only be described as latently homosexual and desperate, or to demonstrate one's disdain by showing the rump. This is also sometimes used as a "support" of other Satanists who are being "attacked" by healthy, reasonable, and mature adversaries. It is also particularly ill-mannered and reminiscent of third-world magical thinking. This is punctuated with a lack of control of one's waist along with a tendency to show one's disdain of rivals with a pants-on, Beavis and Butthead-like backward bow to defy and point out the mannerly and the competent that have forced them into these desperate measures via the soundness of their reason. Digging at one-another's chests with their bat hands as though there were a magical show going on there is another indication, an indication of Satanism and the imminent loss of an argument without those behaviors.

An important and central strategy of this dynamic is visiting the sins of the father on the son. For the Good Father, this is a warning and something to watch for and help with, for the Evil Father, this is a tool of those without fear, shame, and guilt, the evil fathers, to be used against those with shame, fear, and guilt, the sons. In modern terms, it is a form of psychological projection on the part of the evil father and an act of introjection and identification on the part of the son. It is also important to deny that the Good Father made heaven and earth and claim that the material world is "of the devil," and it is only by being in league with the devil ("in charge of the devil") that one will make any money.

They use rhetoric because it is a step below logic. Rhetoric is an earlier discovery of man than logic, and by holding everyone to the standard of rhetoric and spin and decrying good logic, they keep the argument to a more childish mode and prevent reasoned counter arguments and transform the discussion into mere foolish bluster where the loudest, meanest and most obnoxious will win. They thereby deliver the dialog to the foolish, and keep it out of the hands of the mature. The trivium of the ancient Greeks already acknowledged this hierarchy of learning and debate, pointing out that the first development is the discovery of the grammar of language, the second, rhetoric, and the third, logic and that each subsequent one of these is a step higher in the evolution of mind than the previous. The discovery of the trivium is the origin of education and understanding, and using only rhetoric or at least cutting off logical debate is an attack on education and understanding and a refuge for the incompetent, the Satanists.

The try to bamboozle the public into a world of magical thinking by convincing them that if that they vote like the politicians, the pundits and the wealty, they will have the things that politicians, the pundits, and the wealthy have. They convince the people, their serfs, that it is the common perception (misperception) of reality, not reality that makes things work, conveniently neglecting to point out that you pay the rent within reality, not the perception of reality.

In order to maintain this dynamic, they must be able to control the masses. They must keep them in fear and in the dark and must not allow them to vote of their own volition. The will, rights, and intentions of the voters are dismissed as foolish and childish, and it is asserted that they must be controlled for their own good. The safety net is used as an example of all the foolishness of the poor deluded voter. Rather than extolling it as an intelligent tool in the face of the realities of sickness, economic downturn, natural disaster and so on, where the voters decide to pool their money to create a system of welfare, unemployment, social security, Medicare and so on, they demonize it as the theft of the wealth of the nation by dependent losers who merely want to prey on the American family and the government and lay around on a couch taking drugs and borrowing children for the welfare officers visit. They ignore the intelligence of a safety net as they recognize that without it the voter will have much more fear and thereby be much easier to control. They even deny the right of the voter to decide what level of a safety net they want and keep everyone focused on the abuses of the system, while they themselves plunder it, the government, and the worker by taking ever more family-of-four incomes out of the companies, communities and the capitalist economy with the tools of the Satanists. "Who is going to pay for this," they shout. "Certainly, not us," as thousands more voters are pushed into unemployment and worse and while hundreds of thousands of family-of-four incomes pour into the coffers of their personal, aristocrat fiefdoms never to return to capitalism. Moneys that could be used to create and police a proper safety net are lost forever.

If the voter thinks that 2 years of unemployment is appropriate and affordable, it is up to them, not the wealthy or the politicians. The voters are the true authority in America not the wealthy. A safety net is affordable: it very obviously is but the "get the inventor/talent/creator … out" attitude has allowed the wealthy to take the funds and place them in their personal fiefdoms.

The Satanists are against the vote, the voter, and a free thinking public and must not allow them to think through the issues or vote of their own volition. They see the vote as easy to manipulate, and they seek to replace the American government with a "benevolent" aristocracy or a "benevolent" monarchy run by themselves, the Satanists. And if the voter dare get in the way, they will give themselves billions more in bonuses, cut taxes on themselves, and raise ATM fees until we comply. We are not allowed to say "regulate the rich" or "tax the rich." Like the Satanist despots they are, they insist on complete unaccountability and will punish anyone who calls them on it. Phrases such as "democracy doesn't work." "The voter is too easy to manipulate" are typical.

They are against the vote, against the voter, against democracy, against free speech, against the constitution, and against any and all regulation of themselves, the aristocrats. Tthey are not just Satanists, they are traitors. They espouse free speech but between the lines indicate that there is no such thing as free speech, and that the Bible does not support it, clear indications of their disdain for the Constitution, the vote, and the voter.

To identify, isolate, and to remove the Satanists, one need only follow the control and the spin to their source. A good indicator of someone's participation in this dynamic is an effort to be the one "in charge." "In charge," is a term that is used in childhood when a parent, teacher, babysitter, or other guardian needs to be identified wherever a dependent child goes, and the one in charge is the one who is taking the parental role and the authority. In an effort to infantilize the voter, they get the immature to want to be in charge, and then insist that anyone who is not with them is not in charge and instead needs a guardian. This is also a kind of in-charge-pyramid scheme, and there will be someone at the top. There are lots of such pyramids and at the top of them you can find, the politicians, the pundits, and the aristocrats who are driving this attack on freedom and capitalism. Unlike the conscious pyramid represented by the eye of God on the dollar bill, these pyramids are only half conscious at best. They only keep their eyes on the love of money, use the control mechanisms outlined above and go on about the business of creating their personal governments at the expense of all others.

Crucial to identifying them is the lack of shame, fear, and guilt and a never ending need to justify, rationalize, and moralize their behaviors, behaviors that are at the expense of those with normal levels or excessive levels of shame, fear, and guilt. Like all narcissists and perps, they take the lack of shame, fear, and guilt as a justification of their behaviors and a sanction from God, a confirmation of their saintliness, their salvation, their enlightenment or their wisdom, rather than as a warning from Him or as a confirmation from the Evil Father.

The wealthy can also be identified by the frozen, jaded countenances reminiscent of the faces frozen in the ice beneath Dante's feet in the deepest level of hell. They tend to confuse spiritual joy with sadistic grins and schadenfreude. Like gangs, their only criteria for association is fear, spite, and an enjoyment of schadenfreude as they devastate the country and its citizens. They don't like each other or anyone else but manage to get along through targeting, isolating, and harassing a common vic. They cackle, grin, high five, and congratulate each other with each blow they deliver to their vic, all the better if the vic's career and homelife is ruined.

The voter has the right and the duty to tax this money away from the wealthy and the politicians who support them, the Satanists, and put the money back in the hands of those who truly made it, the customers, the employees, and the stockholders. The wealthy did not make this money, they stole it. They merely created a set of financial and legal tools to wrench the money from those who truly earned it.

The wealthy will not apologize for being successful which is good, because they are not. What they should be apologizing for, making peace with God, his country and the voter for is their theft: Tens of thousands of family of four incomes pour into the coffers of their personal fiefdoms every year off the backs of the customers, the employees and the stockholders, and there is only the faintest trickle of family-of-four jobs coming out. They and their like are shameless.

They are shameless, anti-American traitors, and they must be stopped. They must be stopped by a vote that will redistribute the wealth back to those who truly made it, the customers, employees, and stockholders, the creators, inventors, and talent. The voter has a duty and a right to tax the rich thoroughly, profoundly, and punitively. More importantly, it must be recognized that when the wealthy go to the inventors, the creators and the talent and say to them, like the Chinese say to us, "We made that. It was our idea, we merely got you do it for us, and you can go now." We need to recognize that as a Satanist effort sending his minion, Lucifer, to God to take credit for the Creation and take over whatever was created and the profits therefrom.

If we do not stop them, they will only continue until the U.S. is replaced by personal fiefdom's, and the vote is nothing more than a stupid, toothy smile and a bobble headed nod to whatever whim crosses the mind of the wealthy. If we do not stop them, they will send the voter back to their hovels for their cold bowl of soup, and if they dare again to say "regulate the rich" or "tax the rich," they will take that cold bowl of soup and leave them with gravel and weeds. Without a safety net, there is much more fear, and the voter is much easier to manipulate. The vote and the voter are NOT easy to manipulate. The manipulation of the vote requires undoing centuries of progress in civilization, trying to obviate the Bill of Rights, the Constitution, the Declaration and the Magna Carta ... at least. And of course, being those who ignore the lessons, the documents, of history, they will be the ones to repeat them.

Let's not join them. When they say "Get them to vote against the very reasonable ability to pool their money via the tax to create a safety net and you've got them." We can say, "Or so you thought: tax the rich again and again and again until they sit up straight, fold their hands on the table, apologize, and PUT THE MONEY BACK!" The voter is the authority in America, not the wealthy. The creator is the source of the wealth, not the Lucifer, the minion of Satan.

They will continue to take the family-of-four incomes out of the communities, companies, and U.S. economy as long as they are not held responsible. We all know that if the government were given 350,000,000 dollars a year, those 7,000 family-of-four incomes would not stagnate in the coffers of the soi-disant aristocratic lords and their cronies. It would have to be spent, and it would be spent through creating family-of-four jobs that set a standard for work weeks, benefits, and work-place behaviors. There would be no six figure bonuses, no 9 figure annual incomes, and no 25 million dollar severance packages for failed performance. We want our government jobs back. We want our unions back. We want our safety net back. We want our hard earned money back.

They need to be reminded of the power of free speech, the vote, and the U.S. Constitution.

Make or Break the 2012: Tax the Rich!

Philip A. Bralich, Ph.D.

Give me liberty or give me debt. (It's easier this go around.)

http://www.taxtherich.name

Copyright © 2011 Mass Media Distribution LLC - 3350 Riverwood Pkwy Suite 1900 - Atlanta, Georgia 30339

Sitemap | Contact Info | Order Press Release Distribution | MMD Disclaimer | Copyright Notice | Older Press Releases:

SOME NOTES ON ARISTOCRACY:

http://philipbralich.authorsxpress.com/2012/09/08/from-taxtherichdotname-some-notes-on-the-nature-of-aristocray/

From TaxTheRichDotName: Some notes on the nature of aristocray

Posted on September 8, 2012

Some notes on the creeping aristocracy

"In a time of ignorance, one has no doubts even while doing the greatest evils [power politics, political expeditiousness, spin]; in an enlightened age, one trembles even while doing the greatest goods [the Declaration, the Constitution, the Bill of Rights]. One feels the old abuses and sees their correction, but one also sees the abuses of the correction itself."

L'Esprit des Lois ("The Spirit of the Laws"), Montesquieu, Charles de Secondat, baron de 1748.

(Most of the following is just a paraphrase of the above work.)

Forms of Government:

There are only 3 forms of gov't (monarchy (rule by 1), republic (rule by many), and despotism (rule by chaos, dominance and fear)).

1. Monarchy rule by one (w/ a body of laws, an assembly and a counsel but no vote): Runs on the honor of the family of the monarchy, falls on honesty — truth not the current received truth or truthiness.

2. Republic: government by many, either a) an elite (aristocracy, usually landed white males) or b) as many of the people as reasonable (democracy). The aristocratic version of a Republic is run on the family honor of the aristocrats; it also falls around honesty, but this is the whistle blower honesty in MANY companies/families of the aristocrats, not just that of the monarchy (many Voltaires are required). Caste systems, South American Aristocracies, etc are good ideas. You are not be welcomed into the top echelons: you are being welcomed into centuries of serfdom to the aristocracy you are joining.

3. Despotism: No real leadership, just dominance and control where the most vicious will rule as long as they remain the most vicious. Runs on fear, intimidation and the whims of the top dog; falls on fearlessness (TRUE fearlessness not cocksureness, boldness or pretenses to honor and fearlessness.) Anarchy, tyranny, collectivism, communism, and tribalism are good examples as in North Korea, Mao's China, and Hitler's Germany.

Monarchy, aristocracy, and democracy are as much unconscious psychological dynamics as conscious ones: a personal commitment to the dynamic determines the degree to which you will participate.

For an aristocrat, there is a deep sense of ancestors and descendants.

As soon as you involve yourself in that sort of elitism, you will begin to notice your decision making is "of my descendants, for my descendants and by me and my ancestors." It is not for the people, the government, the country others or God, it is all a matter of your personal family lineage. The aristocrat will join with other elitists but only in mutual support of the "of my family, for my family, and by family" dynamic, and all decision making will be more like an armed truce than a consensus or a vote (cf Microsoft). There will be little or no sense of giving back to the U.S. who made it possible, nor God, nor others. Like the TV commercial that says, "We will turn the poor boy into a poor man," all non-members of the elite are "treated" to an invite to the elite which is really a further serfing of non-members. Serfs are targets not people. It takes many, many generations for a serf family (there is no middle class or one that is quite small and diminishing) to move up.

Some Examples of Aristocratic Policy:

Capital gains tax: The Bush descendants will own Texas, the Cheney descendants will own Pennsylvania, etc., "of my family, by my family, and for my family and my family alone" – the armed truce for other aristocrats, serfdom for all others.

Aristocrats are also narcissists with a sociopathic intractability and an unwillingness to be held accountable for anything (as they are "perfect") as in the opening quote. This narcissism explains much of the gridlock and the lack of communication, no matter how well or how dramatically something is said on the left or the right. A constant spinning truthfulness and hearsay keep the serfs riled up on the wrong points, unable to cooperate and coordinate, and at bay.

Bringing down the growing aristocracy in the U.S. is the same as bringing down a monarchy but requires a more diffuse focus on more families/corporations. Starbucks is a particularly good target. Many whistle blowers are required.

Focusing on Romney alone would be an error, though he is a good target. It is also important to include aristocrats in states and corporation,s congress and the senate, wall street etc. The work needs to be divided up. Even in the states the state politicians need to focus on many aristocrats not the top one.

Democracy runs on love of freedom, equality, and love of country; it falls on selfishness and arrogance (an excess of individualism). Equality is not a cockroach like equality where everybody gets the same or "no one gets a violin unless everyone gets a violin": this merely leads to zero orchestras and monstrous crowds of bad violinists. U.S. equality, the quality of a democracy, is one in which the rights of all are protected including those of the talented, the experienced, hard working, and the skilled. That's why we have sports and music and geniuses and inventions and poets and stars who live outside the gulag. That is why control, manipulation, and oppression lead to prison here (except for the anticipated but undealt with problem of a possible, now nearly present, aristocracy).

Philip A. Bralich, Ph.D.

http://www.taxtherich.name or Google TaxTheRichDotName or Philip Bralich

Also: http://www.amazon.com/Common-Cents-Full-Taxtherich dotname-E-mails/dp/1452551391/ref=sr_1_6?ie=UTF8&qid=134 7073479&sr=8-6&keywords=philip+bralich

http://philipbralich.authorsxpress.com/2012/09/02/from-blaming-japhy-rider-thomas-paine-talks-to-invisible-obama/

← Previous Next →

From Blaming Japhy Rider: Thomas Paine Talks to Invisible Obama

Posted on September 2, 2012

#taxtherichdotname #eastwooding

Thomas Paine Talks to Invisible Obama.

T. Paine: So just when are you and your opponents going to stop the silly bickering, backstabbing, nitpicking, and catcalling and do something of value for the people?

Invisible Obama:

T. Paine: No that is not what they want, they want you to win on the issues, not the foolish bickering. They are not fooled by you or the blame.

Invisible Obama:

T. Paine: I just said you should stop that. You are still blaming and the voters don't want that. It is both of your faults. You have to solve the problem and get back to business.

Invisible Obama:

T. Paine: You are still just blaming one another and excusing each other. What is the real problem?

Invisible Obama:

T. Paine: No it is definitely not communism, and it is not fascism: both of those are just variations of despotism. Do you even know the three possible forms of government?

Invisible Obama:

T. Paine: Well, no it is not "democrat, republican, and stupid." It is "monarchy, republic, and despotism," or rule by one, rule by many or rule by none. The last is difficult to see as despotism, but in despotism all leadership is lost to dominance and control and a pack mentality develops where the most vicious will rule, and then only until he is no longer the most vicious, North Korea is a good example as are Hitler and Mao.

Invisible Obama:

T. Paine: That's very astute. A republic has two variations. Both are rule by the many but an Aristocracy is rule by an elite, "a few," while democracy is rule by the many, the people.

Invisible Obama:

T. Paine: No this is not the few and many of who will be chosen. It is the few and many of the parable of God's wedding feast for his son. The wealthy did not turn up as they were too busy and too "sainted," so God invited the democratists, the many. Occasionally, there is one that does not bother to wear his best attempt at wedding clothes, but this is rare.

Invisible Obama:

T. Paine: Well, no knows for sure of course, but it is typical of elite groups to take their wealth as a mark of favor by God but when he refuses to acknowledge this, they shun him and his invitations and wait for him to come to them for elucidation on how to make money rather than miracles.

Invisible Obama:

T. Paine: Yes, indeed, the problem today is neither monarchy nor despotism, it is aristocracy. We saw this as a future danger for the republic (the democratist, "many" republic) given the economic system, but as the problem had not yet arisen, it was difficult to write law to prevent a merely foreseen danger rather than a present one. It is now present.

Invisible Obama:

T. Paine: Well, if you can't figure that out yourself, I'll tell you. A monarchy is brought down by an honest man, one who will not cowtow to the received truth, the" truthiness" of the monarchy. An honest critic, like Voltaire for instance, is devastating to a monarchy. Can you figure out what will bring down an aristocracy?

Invisible Obama:

T. Paine: Yes, again very nice. Many critics criticizing the many aristocrats.

Invisible Obama:

T. Paine: No not criticizing them as a group but criticizing then one by one. It requires more planning and awareness of the dynamic to bring down an aristocracy. For example, the elite will want everyone to focus on one thing or one person which is just a never ending snipe hunt. What they are afraid of is a diffuse focus on a number of the aristocratic families or corporations. For example, while Romney is drawing the focus, the rest will be working in the background, all the while firing up everyone to focus on Romney. You need a few dozen families or corporations to focus on by themselves. This will drain the Romney's and the whole dynamic. It is also best not to connect them with the one big thing or the one big person, just do them individually.

Invisible Obama:

T. Paine: Yes, that is it exactly. Stop mobilizing your forces against one man or the republicans and mobilize them instead against the many aristocrats. Honest, insightful critics divvying up the work at the grassroots level, locally, statewide, and nationally. Diffuse criticism, not focused criticism. Not one person, one thing, or one group.

Invisible Obama:

T. Paine: Well, certainly what you are doing is not working. Let your grassroots people work within the guidelines you have so far provided and let the average voter work as he sees fit, but add the proviso that this diffuse approach will pierce the aristocratic (corporate) veil and allow republicans, democrats, and independents to vote their hearts not their wallets or their fears.

Invisible Obama:

T. Paine: I think you should.

#taxtherichdotname On Goldiggers: those who would compliment, wheedle, control, cowtow, be controlled, etc to the guy who gets where he's going via predation (the Capt'n of the football team, alpha male, the Romney, etc) while targeting and nitpicking the predator protector date, the guy who gets where is going through honesty via the bets "I am your mom or the mom you should have had" degrding and demeaning behaviors. All the while pretending that at some point the target will be good enough , read "Predator enough" to join the ranks of the guys who get gold dug and cheered. This can also be used by women in the workplace. n.b. many women in the news can be seen this way — their own form of media bias — predators only.

John Adams said of Thomas Paine, "Without the pen of Paine the sword of Washington would have been wielded in vain."

"Thomas Paine had taken up writing at middle age; and, in contrast to the pompous style of the 18th century writers, he a...

voided quoting the classics and wrote in the simple language of the people. He saved his money and printed a little pamphlet covering his views on freedom. The pamphlet bore the title Common Sense. It came off the press early in 1776, and in the entire history of printing, there has never been such a spontaneous sale as greeted the appearance of Common Sense. It was not copyrighted; there were no copyright laws, and anyway, Paine wanted no profit from his political writings. The first edition didn't even bear his name. In those early months of 1776 it was printed and reprinted and reprinted, successively, again and again. It has been estimated that, out of a population of 3,000,000 people, more than 300,000 bought copies."

PROBLEMS ACROSS THE AISLE

On Women in the Workplace:

http://philipbralich.authorsxpress.com/2012/08/11/
on-women-in-the-workplace/

← Previous Next →

On Women in the Workplace

Posted on August 11, 2012

From TaxTheRichDotName: On Women in the Work Place or "When She was Good, She was Very, Very, Good …"

On Women in the Work Place

The feminist movement and women in the workplace is hardly new, but it has only really had any success since the 70s, and even after that, we have not had significantly large number of women in the workplace except perhaps for the last 20 or 30 years. We can look at women in the workplace in Communist Russia and China as well as in South America as early experiments, but in Europe and the U.S., we have had a very wide success and very large numbers of women in the workplace in capitalist economies from which to begin a real discussion of the issue.

One of the most important considerations in this discussion is the tremendous support women have had from men since the 70s. Many men from that time and continuing now continue to vote and make efforts toward equal pay for equal work not because they feel bullied into it by anyone or because they feel they have no choice or because they are controlled into it, but merely because they believe it is right and good for the culture and the country. They also work on their own attitudes, being careful not to demean or stereotype and to make sincere efforts to ensure that the principle of "the best person for the job" is adhered to independent not only of gender but of race, color, creed, etc as well. We were convinced early on by the coming off the times in the 70s and by arguments by men and women both on the subject. We continue this support in the same way, because it is right, because of the times and because of the arguments of men and women both.

The women we supported and continue to support, just like the men we supported and continue to support, are those who seek positions and promotion based on their qualifications, talent, and experience independent of group identification, consensus, mutual admiration societies, popular but erroneous opinion, "paying ones dues," membership in pyramid scams or confidence games, mentors (though genuine written references and recommendations are welcome), vigilantism, vigilantism, kangaroo courts, lynch mobs, old boy networks, old girl networks, or old boy and old girl networks. We also do not buy into bad behavior, innuendo, slander, undermining, gossip, threats to our homes or families, pretenses to black magic, perversion, sexual harassment, sexual harassment policies that do not mitigate against the iuse of innuendo and past history, imagined "special" insights into people's characters independent of the resume and common sense, back stabbing, damning with weak praise, scoffing at good work and ideas, cackling, ill manners, crude behaviors (no matter who is blamed for them), the praising of bad work by ones cohort and the damning of good work by competitors, derailing arguments and good speakers who are outside ones cohort, speaking over people, shouting over people, interrupting, and so forth.

That is, we do not support the behaviors of the O'Reilley's, the type-A men, Wall Street sociopaths, right or left wing sociopaths, the Views, the Oprah's, Rosie, Roseann, or the Marthas, all of whom depend on the bad behaviors just described. We are the competent good boy and good girl, mature adults who simply do not see the above behaviors as useful for the workplace, the economy, the culture, or the country, even if they can temporarily provide fortunes, 9 figure annual incomes, and 25 million dollar bonuses for failed performance for a short while. We further do not support any men or women in the workplace who support these behaviors. We simply see equal pay for equal work and many other gender based issues as important, and we support them.

However, that being said, we also recognize that the bad behaviors just described have crept into the work place and while we see no reason to blame either women or men for the problem, it is reasonable to think that some of the problems is coming from the newness of women in the workplace and the as not yet completed adjustment to it.

While many of the failed women in the work place constantly insist on denying the role of men in the success of women have had in the work place, continue to treat all of political and workplace issues as coming from men in their war on men, a phrase which they will not tolerate, as they instead insist there is a war on women. They emasculate men, slander and harass men and women both who dare to be competent, and particularly those who point out to them how transparent their subterfuges and "switcheroos" are. They criticize men for constantly comparing sticks while themselves are constantly comparing pads and trying to emasculate men into constantly comparing pads like the primitives in a matriarchy with its matrons and huts.

When we embarked on this, we supported the competent of all genders, races, creeds, etc, not fat chicks, bull dykes, boney assed white women, transgenders who want to dominate the social scene with their prancing, fat guys with beards who want to tell us that Bugs Bunny and Machu Pichu came from UFOs rather than the mind of man, shrieking derailments of reason and good speakers, the scapegoating of men, particularly competent men, consensus mongerers, control freaks, people who hallucinate across your chest, head, or backside and then demote you because of what they have "seen," or anything of their like.

The competent men and women both recognize that there has not been a whit of appreciation for our efforts in writing, speech, or in the media and recognize that this lack of recognition is a deliberate slight and an attempt to usurp the roles of those who can earn their way without the bad behaviors. We also recognize that this lack of recognition is likely to continue because they know we will do what is right. The war against men is not just a war against men but all the good boy and good girl mature adults who want to do what is right rather than turn the culture wholesale over to the matrons (they call themselves "mentors" and often see themselves as gurus) whose only agenda is to advance themselves in the name of the "bad behavior" of those good boy and good girl mature adults, dismissing all of the positive efforts and their genuine effectiveness in bringing equality to the workplace and also demonizing them as soldiers in or sympathizers with the war on women. These matrons and their cohort are bigots.

However, even though the good boy and good girl mature adults will continue to support, work for, and vote for what is right because it is right, and the matrons will dismiss and take credit for all these efforts, something must be done by the good boy and good girl mature adults to stop the onslaught on our culture by matriarchs and primitivity – primitivity is not new, it is a regression. We have fallen into the trap that Marcuse warned us about back in the 60s. The tolerance of intolerance merely leads to more intolerance. The intolerant swell their imagined ranks with our unwillingness or supposed inability to criticize. Something must be done to give credit where credit is due and to put the blame where the blame belongs, on primitivity.

Sincerely,

Philip A. Bralich, Ph.D.

"… but when she went bad, she was gone."

Prestare il proprio fianco alle critiche.

On Heterophobia:

http://philipbralich.authorsxpress.com/2012/08/11/
on-heterophobia-civil-unions-gay-marriage/

On Heterophobia, Civil Unions & Gay Marriage

Posted on August 11, 2012

On Heterophobia, Gay Marriage and Civil Unions

(Heterophobia = fear of one's own or other's healthy dating behaviors, fertility, or healthy, viable 20-something appearances.)

There are two facts about homosexuality that all sane people will agree to: 1) that no culture exists that does not have some number of gays in its population either openly or clandestinely and 2) that "gay bashing" negatively impacts the culture with vigilantism and the injury and death of gays as well as those falsely accused (either through naiveté and superstition or through deliberate slander – there are even cultures that claim they can recognize homosexuals at birth and practice infanticide in the name of this "vision").

The vigilantism is not only overt but also passive-aggressive, and it permeates the culture with an obsessive testing and faking of homosexual behaviors that have no other effect but to guarantee the homophobic and heterophobic advantages in the workplace guaranteeing that the inappropriate will always have an edge. Some of those who are targeted are completely without real or imagined homosexual behavior markers, but merely refuse to participate in those obsessive, ever-present, latently homosexual, inappropriate behaviors and perverted, pimpy pantomimes in the name of a true commitment to politically correct behaviors, appropriateness, and a workplace and community without sexual harassment. These are truly heterosexual and they frighten both many of the heterophobic and the homophobic. Those who refuse to participate in the inappropriateness are victims of heterophobia and are often harassed out of the workplace and community or forced to comply with the inappropriateness. This subtler, passive-aggressive form of vigilantism is often used to harass the competent as well – those who can make their way in the work place without the perverted, pimpy behaviors are simply made targets of both heterophobia and homophobia. Anyone who dare be both competent and appropriate is the first and major target for mobbing and bullying in any workplace or community plagued by homophobia and heterophobia. One of the signs of the deliberateness and consciousness of these efforts is the removal of prohibitions against innuendo (slander, gossip, and hearsay) and sexual past history as important provisions in the sexual harassment policy.

While homosexuals in the U.S. have gained a wider acceptance and wider protection, there are those who refuse to believe that strong negative reactions to homosexuality are as inevitable in any culture as homosexuality is itself . There are also those who insist that one is either 100% pro-homosexual rights or 100% against them. The gay community needs to deal with the reality that many will never give up their negative associations to homosexuality as inevitably as there will always be gays in any culture. And they can no more be 100%"educated" out of the culture as homosexuality could. Certainly education helps, but it cannot be one-sided, the reality of the existence of gays needs to be taught to others as much as the reality and inevitability of those who will never accept it. All we can really hope to do is quiet the violence and encourage civility in a long-term process. And those gays who prefer to educate the culture need to recognize and accept that there will always be those who want to educate them. There is no reason the educators from both sides cannot sit down and have a sane and reasonable discussion about their differences and no reason members of both sides cannot attend the other sides' classes with an open mind to see what they have to say: knee jerk reactions, shouting, and flaunting should be avoided.

One particularly good example of the homosexual community's refusal to accept the inevitability of this opinion in any culture is their refusal to recognize there are many democrats and many liberals who do not and will never accept it and are often forced into "hiding" in the right wing to affect their agenda from there rather than be intimidated by the constant bombardment of democratic rallies with transgender parades and the most exaggerated homosexual behaviors in the face of all and any other democratic issues (except perhaps abortion which is equally exaggerated in its popularity and its expediency as a liberal issue and identifier). Adherents of both issues insist that anyone who is not 100% for the latest and greatest and most extreme of all the homosexual hot-button issues or abortion issues today simply must not be a liberal. Extremists adherents of both issues have decimated the left and this fact is totally unrecognized. Certainly both sides are completely unaware of the effectiveness of subtler and slower, more considered approaches to these issues that may have more effective results for those two main issues than the extremes could ever effect.

Returning to the original issue that sane people agree that all cultures will have homosexuality and that the vigilantism in its wake is not of value to the culture; neither liberals nor conservatives can allow the extremes of these issues to polarize and dominate American politics to the degree that they do, and they must realize that effective policy for all would be more likely to result if the extremists were not so determined to dominate the left and America with just those two issues and we could return to sane and reasonable discussion of many issues.

The issue of gay marriage is once again "in the face" of the 2012 political candidates distracting them and forcing them to be labeled either anti-gay or anti-God when there are many other issues that need to be addressed.

TaxTheRichDotName is itself on a one-issue mission and as such will take no side on this issue, but would like to point out that a number of states do allow gay marriage or civil unions, so why not step back for a few months and see whether the passage of these laws have a positive or negative effect on those two main issues: the refusal to recognize the reality of homosexuality in any culture and the vigilantism that affects everyone (particularly the competent) if it takes root.

Sincerely,

Philip A. Bralich, Ph.D.

Give me liberty or give me debt: It is easier this go around.

Metaphor:

Characterizing liberals as baby killing, trans-genders with no other political agenda than to impose kneepads and a ring and a slot for a three-dollar bill in every register in America on all Americans is a lot like characterizing conservatives as the party of toe-tapping Larry Craig's bottom feeding their "power" from the bus stop bathrooms of

America with no other political agenda than to leave their demented, bi-polar, pregnant, 16-year-old daughters with no other recourse to "resolve" their terror than a fat chick with a coat hanger looking to create more Sybil's and the pack of jackals that would be necessary to protect such a demoness, such a Whore of Babylon.

On the Legalization of Devil Weed:

http://philipbralich.authorsxpress.com/2012/06/13/
on-the-legalization-of-devil-weed/

On the Legalization of Devil Weed

Posted on June 13, 2012

On the Legalization of Devil Weed

One of the greatest tools for the effective manipulation of a voting populace is hot button issues: abortion, legalization of drugs and prostitution, Obama's birth certificate. Some of these are crucially important to the culture and to the voter while others are just trivial, but either way they are shamelessly used by the politicians to distract the voter from a full, complete, and coherent platform in order to maintain gridlock and the wealth and momentum of the creeping aristocracy, to keep the voters from asking for a full platform, and primarily to keep them off the one, hot-button issue that really matters, the distribution of wealth, which itself has a myriad of hot-button distracters to keep sanity and redistribution from actually occurring: flat tax, abolish all tax, sales-tax-only are issues that are going to keep blowing in the wind for decades preventing an intelligent solution and preventing the voter from approaching the Luciferian efforts of the wealthy to get the companies and the profits from the inventors, the creatives, and the talent; that is, a solution that provides a profound, thorough, and punitive tax on the wealthy, one that is implemented nearly immediately and redone over and over and over again until the Luciferian Creeping Aristocracy sits up straight, folds their hands nicely on the table, admits they were wrong, apologizes and puts the money back. And further, to continue the pressure until the politicians always have an easily implemented tax the rich bill at the ready for anytime the creeping aristocracy tries again to spread the wings of that nine-headed dragon in order to gouge the voter. And further still, until the history books and economic books read that the rich learned their lesson, and that the economy needs to be grounded in the creatives and the family of four income not the bottom line.

The legalization of drugs, particularly of marijuana, however, is more than just a hot-button issue used to keep the public away from what matters. It is an issue that has imminent, on-going, and potential negative impact on individuals and on the culture overall. The debate is fueled and rendered ineffective by both its use as a detractor from more crucial issues and by the problem itself, the illogic and deludedness that result from marijuana use. Since the 60s users have wanted to legalize the drug and have effectively (and correctly) reduced the penalties for its use; however, the movement is incapable of recognizing or admitting the devastating effects of this drug, which start early on with the jaded, dark-green glasses that turn up almost immediately after one takes it up. In high school and even younger, as soon as marijuana use becomes a factor all other activities seem uncool, conservative plots to take over the minds of the youth, and the users insist that boy scouts, girl scouts, extra-curricular activities, school politics, part time jobs, in short anything that does not come with bad clothes, bad music, and the occasional skateboard is seen as dumb and an attraction for nerds, not the cool kids. They fail to recognize that soon after the use begins, the users lose the ability to turn up at meetings, participate meaningfully, or to get along with others who do not fully condone drug use. This is confused by the few who actually can maintain and by those who have one of the few "accepted" disciplines within the users community such as bands and guitars. The bands and guitars provide a discipline that allow the user to maintain some semblance of sanity through the laziness, dismissiveness, and jadedness of the typical user and even worse puts the musicians in a position to treat their audiences as drones and to futher their numbers by pretending to support the bat-handed, shaken-baby head bobbing, bad clothes and dronishness of their near slave fans. The fns become compliant and loyal as long as the message is the one that supports the dark green, jaded-glasses that leave them nothing else to do but air guitar their songs, go to the their concerts, and buy their records and t-shirts. The drones lose their ability to attract the opposite sex or to impress them and they resort to further rationalizations and insistence that their dates take drugs as well and rather than recognizing this inability to date, they resort to manipulation, control, and pimp behaviors in order to force someone to be a partner. This is further reinforced by metaphysical excuse making where the delusions, demi-hallucinations, and frank hallucinations are treated as some sort of underworld shamanism and as a wisdom that simply cannot be questioned either among themselves or from outsiders (largely because this "wisdom" is painfully transparent as to what it truly is, fool's gold folly). Their piggish behaviors and dominance, in the true blame-the-victim mentality of a rapist or pimp are blamed on the unenlightened "rabble" who do not have the good sense to "enhance" their vision with the paranoid deludedness of the drug. The users quickly go from those who can participate in life, make decisions, learn and create into pathetic, marijuana masturbators constantly reaching for metaphysical and political conspiracy excuse making to rationalize their ineffectiveness.

While the above is painfully obvious to the rest of the culture that does not take drugs, the only evidence of an awareness of the problem on the part of the user is only an unconscious tendency to dress up like pre-pubescent, good boys and girls in their team jerseys, baggy pants, and backward caps shouting jovially at their TV screens and reminiscing a more wholesome America, (a time before their drug use began in puberty). Their marijuana, masturbation, and metaphysical excuse making are all bolstered by their further marijuana use and they live in a world dominated by their delusions of being underworld "shamans" managing the demons of others (certainly not their own). They lose their ability to "shamanize" the upper world and are all lost in the never ending back and forth of spells, demons, and sinister plots of the primitive mentality of the third-world, unmodified by the good shamans ability to transform this and the lower world via their upper world visions.

Certainly, putting people into jail for decades for casual use or experimentation is not an answer, but neither is whole scale legalization as this would lead to more and more of such deludedness and less and less of a willingness and ability to combat it. The legalization would not take the "rebel yell" out of the whole thing as the rebel yell is itself one of the symptoms of use whether that use be legally sanctioned or not. The police and the courts and the medical profession need to work together to find effective penalties that would deter its use and effective means for education to point out that the jaded, dark-green glasses and the inability to socialize are not symptomatic of wisdom but of deterioration of the thought process.

It is also necessary for the authorities to undermine the supply and this would most effectively be done by destroying the decades old networks that support its distribution, networks that exist not only along the border but in the jadedness and desire for drones of entrenched public figures (many former users themselves), members of the community, and so forth perhaps even to the House and Senate themselves, the baby boomer hippies now being of that age. The best way to undermine these decades old connections is to clean up not the border, but the border towns on this side of the border, and then, establish patrols to prevent them recurring. It took decades to build up; it will take decades to rebuild. Sweeping the border towns and jailing or sending back thousands of legal and illegal members of these towns will dry up the supply, disrupt the corrupt payments, and seriously disturb the hierarchies of the gangs and entrenched networks on both sides of the border. There will not be "another one there to take his place in a few days" as there will be a need to replaces thousands as well as the networks around the drugs that support them.

Philip A. Bralich, Ph.D

On Media Bias:

http://philipbralich.authorsxpress.com/2012/08/16/
from-taxtherichdotname-on-media-bias/

← Previous Next →

From TaxTheRichDotName: On Media Bias

Posted on August 16, 2012

On the Lesser of the Many Evils

Voters today and perhaps for several decades are forced to choose candidates for their parties that can only be described as the lesser of the many of the evils. Our party loyalties remain strong, and we do what we can throughout politicians tenures and campaigns to "lessen-up" the evil. No party has ever put forth a flawless or perfect candidate but the evils we have had to lessen were for already far less. Once the candidates are chosen, we swallow our disappointments and support them. The noisy crowds of the convinced obscure this as they seem to be actually buying the personality of the candidate. However, throughout the country and on both sides, what drives politics today is party and policy loyalties and not the cults of personality. As these very present but poorly representative crowds make this cheap form of news while the majority of American's do not, the media focus is there. This is an unfortunate fall-out from excessive commercialization of the press which has led to the O'Reilley's and the Views and all the truly reprehensible examples of journalistic abuse. There is a media bias but it is neither liberal nor conservative, it is a bias toward the stupid, the most noise and against the silent majority – the silent majority on both sides of the aisle who just don't make that kind of news. Thus the tawdry displays that are driving the media into a never ending, ever growing contest for greater and greater numbers is actually only generating greater and greater displays, more and more frustrated, quiet mature and high school educated adults and a constant excuse making by the media of these displays and dismissals of the educated and mature audiences.

The anger of the audiences is growing (as well as that of the mature press pressed into the service of the tawdry, just so someone, anyone might be there to ameliorate the damage). The hot button issues that not only dumb down the media but also forces more and more adults into this foolish thinking and the growing anger of the true mainstream audiences – those who don't need tawdry displays, demeaning gestures and pantomimes, and screaming spin know they are being ignored, dismissed, and treated like children and worse, and they know their numbers are dwindling due to this dynamic in the press, in the congress, in the presidential campaigns and pretty much anywhere you look. The possibility of protest is dominated by the ineffective, and the last remaining pressure valves are beginning to weaken and the press and the congress only see this as a possible source of noisier news and a gridlock than can only be seen as guaranteeing the politician a gutless excuse to do as he damn well pleases.

The larger audience is a mature one. Play to them and the O'Reilleys and Views will fall. The cheap entertainment is not fun or funny anymore. It has to stop, the pen digging at the chest of the mature audience is infuriating and deliberately insulting and is meant to feed the shilling audiences of the tawdry while driving away the mature. It will work if something isn't done. Genuine effective action needs to be taken that will return us to a mature, maturing, inspiring, motivating press of times past. O'Reilleys assumption that Americans are stupid and need his brand of "educating" is most insulting of all.

The press and the politicians both need to conspire to get this garbage off the air.

Sincerely,

Philip A. Bralich, Ph.D.

My Demented Fat Aunt, My Slender Poised Aunt

http://philipbralich.authorsxpress.com/2012/08/15/
excerpt-from-the-poetic-selections-my-demented-
fat-aunt-my-slender-poised-aunt/

Excerpt from the Poetic Selections: My Demented Fat Aunt My Slender Poised Aunt

Posted on August 15, 2012

My Demented Fat Aunt, My Slender Poised Aunt

I was raised Catholic in a family with six siblings. My father was from a family of 10 siblings, my mother of 4. They all got married and had lots of Catholic kids. We would frequently get together in our many big back yards where the men would drink beer, the women would chat and the many, many cousins would romp and play.

My demented fat aunt would always be watching the boys: she was terribly concerned that they were masturbating and wanted them to confess to her in great detail what they were doing. My slender poised aunt was always on the lookout for her and would warn the boys not to tell her the slightest thing even if such an unfortunate thing were to occur.

My demented fat aunt forgot that Catholics had priests and confessions or perhaps she thought that somehow she knew better than the priests. My demented fat aunt constantly was saying that she knew what the boys did and wanted them to confess in detail and only she could show them what to do. She would try to teach gross behaviors as a cure. My slender poised aunt would encourage the boys to sit up straight, play nice and be fair. My demented fat aunt wanted to tell the boys that she should arrange their dates and she would undoubtedly fix them up with lazy girls who didn't want to try and jobs that were well below their ability. She said they were following the scent of money and that the weight gain and lack of makeup were the result of that. As soon as the money came they would clean up good. (I thought they were smelling the scent of butt and would only end up in latrines, but I never spoke like that in front of my slender poised aunt. My girlfriends and students hardly know I am capable of speaking like that.) My slender poised aunt would tell the boys that you win girls' hearts with gentlemanly behaviors and interesting accomplishments.

When it came time to look for a girlfriend and go to the prom, my fondness for my slender poised aunt caused me to look for slender poised girls.

My parents seemed totally unaware of this and seemed to like both aunts equally or at least seemed to have little choice in the matter. I thought I caught my mother tearing up when she saw my slender poised aunt one time, but I was quickly redirected to a game of go fish. One time I saw my demented fat aunt wipe her brow toward my mother as if to say, "Phew that was close." I was quickly redirected to a group of kids who were picking raspberries in my grandfather's victory garden.

From *Blaming Japhy Rider: The Email Chronicles* (p. 83)

A possible subtitle may have read "Predator Protection Proms" where gentlemanly behaviors and interesting accomplishments obviate the need to hint or imply what one might want beyond high school (of course overt discussions of college, the military, or going into your father's business were allowed.) Dating the one most likely to stay with predator protection rather than the most popular is the best life-skill. Who knows you may even like the predator protector dates.

Sincerely

Philip A. Bralich, Ph.D.

SOLUTIONS

A Presidential Platform That Anyone Can Understand:

http://philipbralich.authorsxpress.com/2012/08/13/a-petition-for-a-presidetial-platform-anyone-can-understand/

A Petition for a Presidetial Platform Anyone Can Understand

Posted on August 13, 2012

A Presidential Platform Anyone Can Understand

http://www.thepetitionsite.com/858/476/728/a-presidential-platform-anyone-can-understand/

The U.S. citizand and voter is well aware that either of the parties could be offering a full platform in language that anyone can understand, and that in the last 25 years or so we have been given empty rhetoric, hot-button issues, and obfuscation instead of a proper platform written in language that anyone can understand. In spite of this very evident understanding on the part of the voter, we have been told to believe that the world has become too complex for those without MBAs, law degrees and priviledge and are expected to accept the lack of plain language platforms . This final insult to the intelligence of the American public motivates this petitition to all members of congress to support a bill to require political candidates to provide platforms that can be understood by the average high school graduate and make them easily available to the public ...

http://www.thepetitionsite.com/858/476/728/a-presidential-platform-anyone-can-understand/

A Petition to MoC and Appropriate Committees to Sponsor Resolution, Bill, and Amendment to Tax The Rich:

http://philipbralich.authorsxpress.com/2012/08/13/petition-moc-to-support-resolution-bill-to-tax-the-rich/

THE LAISSEZ FAIRE CLAUSE:

http://philipbralich.authorsxpress.com/2012/08/14/
from-taxtherichdotname-the-laissez-faire-clause/

← Previous Next →

From TaxTheRichDotName:
The "Laissez-faire" Clause

Posted on August 14, 2012

Petition to stop the tyranny of the MBAs, Lawyers, and Priviledged via Tax the Rich Legislation

http://www.thepetitionsite.com/takeaction/604/628/925/

http://www.thepetitionsite.com/858/476/728/a-presidential-platform-anyone-can-understand/

Taxation without Representation is Tyranny (even when it is by the priviledged, the MBAs and Lawyers)

TaxTheRichDotName

527 or PAC (e.g. groups primarily created to influence election of candidates for public office)

Legislative Agenda

A Resolution, A Bill, and a Constitutional Amendment to Tax The Rich

The Laisseze-faire Clause is quite important:

Laissez-faire clause: "WHERAS, the vision of the founding fathers saw the wisdom of a Laissez-faire economy which would legislate only for the protection of property rights and against theft and aggression [including that by the privileged, MBAs and lawyers]; now, therefore, be it ...

Mission: TaxTheRichDotName is a grass roots tax watch organization which seeks to inform voters of taxation issues in hopes of bringing about tax law reform and a correction to the current distribution of wealth. The excesses of the distribution of wealth in this country have penetrated into our government so deeply that nothing short of piracy will cut through the mess and find a fair and equitable distribution of wealth. The system is no longer fair, but we can use the system, the vote, to both redistribute the wealth and return the system to a fair one. The tax system is not solely about what is a fair tax: it is about the distribution of wealth which currently favors the rich to levels not seen since Peronist Argentina or King George of the revolutionary era. The voters can change this without seeking the permission or the support of the creeping aristocracy. The voters first and their elected officials second are the true authorities in the U.S., and they can and will take this decision out of the hands of the privileged, the MBAs, the lawyers, and even the elected officials via the vote. The only obstacle to putting the voters back in control is the politician's unwillingness to put the necessary tax the rich bills before congress. To help put these bills before congress and to get a tax the rich plank on the 2012 ballot, all we need is a presence. The politicians would prefer to fear the voters, their constituents, yet they must deal with political realities as well, realities such as the "creeping aristocracy" and the lobbyists. To give them a leg up, we need to demonstrate our presence and our resolve. With a unified tax the rich voice, presence, and effort, we can let them know that we are on their side and willing to stop the gridlock and the creeping aristocracy. We can start with the Resolution, Bill, and Constitutional Amendment that was just sent to appropriate members of congress and appropriate congressional committees and presented just below.

https://www.popvox.com/orgs/ttrdn

Campaign: A Resolution, A Bill, and a Constitutional Amendment to Tax The Rich

The Texts:

A Resolution to Return the U.S. Economy to a Free Market Economy via Bills to Regulate the Wealthy

(1st Draft)

WHEREAS, an elite, aristocratic, wealth based class has developed in the United States with legal and financial tools to wrest companies and/ or their profits from their owners and the employees and stockholders that developed those companies via spurious, expeditious, excessively obtuse and obfuscated tax laws which leave the wealthy under-taxed and nearly unaccountable; and

WHEREAS, an individualist, free-man, family-of-four income has lost its place as the grounding principle of the economy of the nation and been replaced by the wealth based aristocratic notion of the bottom line; and

WHEREAS, the Marxist sense of Capitalism (that of both the aristocratic holder of capital and the creators of capital) has risen up to replace free enterprise and the free market, thereby becoming a tyranny of the few; and

WHEREAS, the true authorities of the nation, the voters and their elected representatives have had their authority nearly usurped by this Marxist, capital based aristicocracy

; now, therefore, be it

RESOLVED, By the Congress here assembled that a bill to tax the rich be passed to address this disparity and all laws contrary to the spirit of this resolution be rescinded.

A Bill to Reestablish a Free Market Economy

BE IT ENACTED BY THE CONGRESS HERE ASSEMBLED THAT:

Section 1. A 15% sur-tax on the upper 30% of the wealthy be passed to address the growing economic tyranny and disparity of wealth in the U.S.

Section 2. A guarantee that this wealth will go one-third toward the payment of the national debt, one-third toward a clearly established cabinet committee of the "safety net," and one-third toward small business development.

Section 3. A cabinet level committee of the safety-net be established to both establish standards and procedures for the establishment and maintenance of unions, minimum and maximum wages, unemployment, health insurance, welfare, social security, pensions, benefits packages, bonuses and severance packages; these standards and procedures as well as to police these standards and procedures and their enforcement.

SECTION 4. This law will take effect within sixty days of passage.

Section 5. All laws in conflict with this legislation are hereby declared null and void.

A Resolution Amending the Constitution to Have
a Tax The Rich Bill Ever at the Ready in Case an
Aristocracy Develops within the U.S. Government

(1st Draft)

WHEREAS, ; an elite, aristocratic, wealth based class has developed in the United States using legal and financial tools to wrest companies and/or their profits from their owners and the employees and stockholders that developed those companies via spurious, expeditious, excessively obtuse and obfuscated tax laws which leave the wealthy under-taxed and nearly unaccountable and free to plunder poorer and less powerful companies; and

WHEREAS, an individualist, free-man, family-of-four income has lost its place as the grounding principle of the economy of the nation and been replaced by the wealth based aristocratic notion of the bottom line; and

WHEREAS, the Marxist sense of Capitalism (that of both the aristocratic holder of capital and the creators of capital) has risen up to replace free enterprise and the free market, thereby becoming a tyranny of the few; and

WHEREAS, the true authorities of the nation, the voters and their elected representatives have had their authority nearly usurped by this Marxist, capital based aristicocracy

WHERAS, the vision of the founding fathers saw the wisdom of a Laissez-faire economy which would legislate only for the protection of property rights and against theft and aggression.

; now, therefore, be it

RESOLVED, By two-thirds of the Congress here assembled, that the following article is proposed as an amendment to the Constitution of the United States, which shall be valid to all intents and purposes as part of the Constitution when ratified by the legislatures of three-fourths of the several states within seven years from the date of its submission by the Congress: - ARTICLE -

SECTION 1: The congress shall have at the ready a tax bill to tax the wealthy ever at the ready should an aristocracy once again try to usurp the true authority of the voter and their elected representatives and the profits of the free enterprise system from their true, inventors, owners, employees, and stockholders.

SECTION 2: The Congress shall have power to enforce this article by appropriate legislation.

...

For more, go to

https://www.popvox.com/orgs/ttrdn

Sincerely,

Philip A. Bralich, Ph.D.